To
My Husband

First published in Great Britain by
Michael Joseph Limited
52 Bedford Square, London WC1
1979

ISBN: 0 7181 1850 2

Printed and bound in Italy by
Arnoldo Mondadori Company Limited

Also by Celia Haddon

A CHRISTMAS POSY

CONTENTS

[3]

St. Valentine's Day

Hail Bishop Valentine, whose day this is,
All the air is thy diocese,
And all the chirping choristers
And other birds are thy parishioners.
Thou marryest every year
The lyric lark, and the grave whispering dove,
The sparrow that neglects his life for love,
The household bird with the red stomacher.
Thou mak'st the blackbird speed as soon
As doth the goldfinch or the halcyon;
The husband cock looks out, and straight is sped,
And meets his wife, which brings her feather bed.
This day more cheerfully than ever shine,
This day, which might inflame thyself, Old Valentine.

JOHN DONNE

Love Will Find Out The Way

Over the mountains
And over the waves,
Under the fountains
And under the graves;
Under floods that are deepest,
Which Neptune obey,
Over rocks that are steepest,
Love will find out the way.

You may esteem him
A child for his might;
Or you may deem him
A coward for his flight;
But if she whom Love doth honour
Be concealed from the day—
Set a thousand guards upon her,
Love will find out the way.

ANONYMOUS, 17th century

SINCERITY.

LOVE'S PHILOSOPHY

The fountains mingle with the river
And the rivers with the ocean,
The winds of heaven mix for ever
With a sweet emotion;
Nothing in the world is single;
All things by a law divine
In one spirit meet and mingle.
Why not I with thine?

See the mountains kiss high heaven
And the waves clasp one another;
No sister-flower would be forgiven
If it disdained its brother,
And the sunlight clasps the earth
And the moonbeams kiss the sea:
What is all this sweet work worth
If thou kiss not me?

PERCY BYSSHE SHELLEY

Upon Her Feet

Her pretty feet
Like snails did creep
A little out, and then,
As if they started at Bo-Peep,
Did soon draw in again.

ROBERT HERRICK

AN OFFERING OF LOVE.

The Passionate Shepherd
To His Love

Come live with me and be my Love,
And we will all the pleasures prove
That hills and valleys, dales and fields,
Or woods or steepy mountain yields.

And we will sit upon the rocks,
And see the shepherds feed their flocks
By shallow rivers, to whose falls
Melodious birds sing madrigals.

And I will make thee beds of roses
And a thousand fragrant posies;
A cap of flowers, and a kirtle
Embroider'd all with leaves of myrtle.

A gown made of the finest wool
Which from our pretty lambs we pull;
Fair-linéd slippers for the cold,
With buckles of the purest gold.

A belt of straw and ivy-buds
With coral clasps and amber studs:
And if these pleasures may thee move,
Come live with me and be my Love.

CHRISTOPHER MARLOWE

THE ENDLESS

KNOT of LOVE.

A SONNET FROM THE PORTUGESE

How do I love thee? Let me count the ways.
I love thee to the depth and breadth and height
My soul can reach, when feeling out of sight
For the ends of Being and ideal Grace.
I love thee to the level of every day's
Most quiet need, by sun and candle-light.
I love thee freely, as men strive for Right;
I love thee purely, as men turn from Praise.
I love thee with the passion put to use
In my old griefs, and with my childhood's faith.
I love thee with a love I seemed to lose
With my lost saints, —I love thee with the breath,
Smiles, tears, of all my life! —and, if God choose,
I shall but love thee better after death.

ELIZABETH BARRETT BROWNING

On A Little Dog Presented To A Lady

This dog may kiss your hand, your lip,
Lie in your lap, and with you sleep,
On the same pillow rest his head,
Be your companion in your bed.
Now he that gave it doth not crave
Any reward of what he gave;
But he would think himself more blest
If you'd but use him as a beast.

ANONYMOUS, 17th century

Love's Offering

My True Love

My true love hath my heart and I have his,
By just exchange one for another given;
I hold his dear, and mine he cannot miss,
There never was a better bargain driven.
My true love hath my heart and I have his.

His heart in me keeps him and me in one,
My heart in him his thoughts and senses guides;
He loves my heart, for once it was his own,
I cherish his, because in me it bides.
My true love hath my heart and I have his.

SIR PHILIP SIDNEY

TRULY THINE

TO HIS COY MISTRESS

Had we but World enough, and Time,
This coyness, lady, were no crime.
We would sit down, and think which way
To walk, and pass our long Love's day.
Thou by the Indian Ganges side
Should'st rubies find: I by the tide
Of Humber would complain. I would
Love you ten years before the Flood:
And you should if you please refuse
Till the Conversion of the Jews.
My vegetable Love should grow
Vaster than empires, and more.slow.
An hundred years should go to praise
Thine eyes, and on thy forehead gaze.
Two hundred to adore each breast:
But thirty thousand to the rest.
An Age at least to every part,
And the last Age should show your heart.
For, lady, you deserve this state;
Nor would I love at lower rate.

But at my back I always hear
Times wingéd chariot hurrying near:
And yonder all before us lie
Deserts of vast Eternity.
Thy Beauty shall no more be found,
Nor, in thy marble vault, shall sound
My echoing song: then worms shall try
That long preserv'd virginity:
And your quaint Honour turn to dust;
And into ashes all my Lust.
The grave's a fine and private place,
But none I think do there embrace.

Now therefore, while the youthful hue
Sits on thy skin like morning dew,
And while thy willing soul transpires
At every pore with instant fires,
Now let us sport us while we may;
And now, like am'rous birds of prey,
Rather at once our Time devour,
Than languish in his slow-chapt power.
Let us roll all our strength, and all
Our sweetness, up into one ball:
And tear our pleasures with rough strife,
Thorough the iron gates of Life.
Thus, though we cannot make our sun
Stand still, yet we will make him run.

ANDREW MARVELL

Jenny Kissed Me

Jenny kiss'd me when we met,
Jumping from the chair she sat in;
Time, you thief, who love to get
Sweets into your list, put that in!
Say I'm weary, say I'm sad,
Say that health and wealth have miss'd me,
Say I'm growing old, but add,
Jenny kiss'd me.

LEIGH HUNT

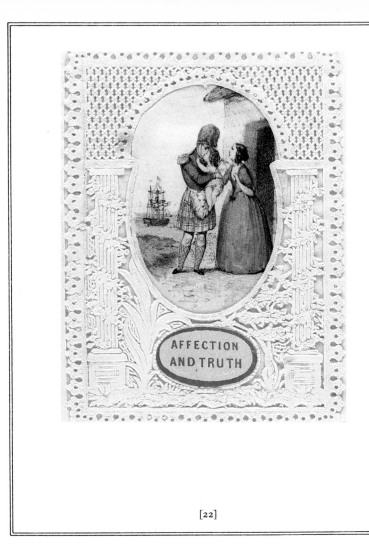

AFFECTION AND TRUTH

To Lucasta

Tell me not, Sweet, I am unkind,
That from the nunnery
Of thy chaste breast and quiet mind,
To war and arms I fly.

True; a new mistress now I chase,
The first foe in the field;
And with a stronger faith embrace
A sword, a horse, a shield.

Yet this inconstancy is such
As you too shall adore;
I could not love thee, Dear, so much,
Lov'd I not Honour more.

Sir Richard Lovelace

TO...

When I loved you, I can't but allow
I had many an exquisite minute;
But the scorn that I feel for you now
Hath even more luxury in it!

Thus, whether we're on or we're off,
Some witchery seems to await you;
To love you is pleasant enough,
But oh! 'tis delicious to hate you!

THOMAS MOORE

SONG

Of all the torments, all the cares,
With which our lives are curst;
Of all the plagues a lover bears,
Sure rivals are the worst!
By partners, in each other kind,
Afflictions easier grow;
In Love alone we hate to find
Companions of our woe.

Sylvia, for all the pangs you see,
Are lab'ring in my breast;
I beg not you would favour me,
Would you but slight the rest!
How great so e'er your rigours are,
With them alone I'll cope;
I can endure my own Despair,
But not another's Hope.

WILLIAM WALSH

Bright Star

Bright star! would I were steadfast as thou art—
Not in lone splendour hung aloft the night
And watching, with eternal lids apart,
Like nature's patient, sleepless Eremite,
The moving waters at their priestlike task
Of pure ablution round earth's human shores,
Or gazing on the new soft fallen mask
Of snow upon the mountains and the moors—
No—yet still steadfast, still unchangeable,
Pillow'd upon my fair love's ripening breast,
To feel for ever its soft fall and swell,
Awake for ever in a sweet unrest,
Still, still to hear her tender-taken breath,
And so live ever—or else swoon to death.

JOHN KEATS

There Is A Lady

There is a Lady sweet and kind,
Was never face so pleased my mind;
I did but see her passing by,
And yet I love her till I die.

Her gesture, motion, and her smiles,
Her wit, her voice, my heart beguiles,
Beguiles my heart, I know not why,
And yet I love her till I die.

Cupid is wingéd and doth range,
Her country so my love doth change:
But change she earth, or change she sky,
Yet will I love her till I die.

ANONYMOUS, 17th Century

[29]

FROM

THE PRINCESS

Now sleeps the crimson petal, now the white;
Nor waves the cypress in the palace walk;
Nor winks the gold fin in the porphyry font:
The fire-fly wakens: waken thou with me.

Now droops the milkwhite peacock like a ghost,
And like a ghost she glimmers on to me.

Now lies the Earth all Danaë to the stars,
And all thy heart lies open unto me.

Now slides the silent meteor on, and leaves
A shining furrow, as thy thoughts in me.

Now folds the lily all her sweetness up,
And slips into the bosom of the lake:
So fold thyself, my dearest, thou, and slip
Into my bosom and be lost in me.

ALFRED, LORD TENNYSON

AFFECTION'S OFFERING.

In A Gondola

The moth's kiss, first!
Kiss me as if you made believe
You were not sure, this eve,
How my face, your flower, had pursed
Its petals up; so, here and there
You brush it, till I grow aware
Who wants me, and wide ope I burst.

The bee's kiss, now!
Kiss me as if you entered gay
My heart at some noonday,
A bud that dares not disallow
The claim, so all is render'd up,
And passively its shatter'd cup
Over your head to sleep I bow.

ROBERT BROWNING

To Her I Love.

Sweet are the charms
of her I love,
More fragrant than the
damask rose,
Soft as the down of turtle
dove,
Gentle as air when Zephyr
blows,
Refreshing as descending rains
To sun-burnt climes and thirsty
plains.

To Mary

I sleep with thee and wake with thee,
And yet thou art not there;
I fill my arms with thoughts of thee—
And press the common air.
Thy eyes are gazing upon mine
When thou art out of sight,
My lips are always touching thine
At morning, noon, and night.

I think and speak of other things
To keep my mind at rest,
But still to thee my memory clings
Like love in woman's breast.
I hide it from the world's wide eye
And think and speak contrary;
But soft the wind comes from the sky
And whispers tales of Mary.

The night wind whispers in my ear,
The moon shines in my face;
A burden still of clinging fear
I find in every place.
The breeze is whispering in the bush,
And the dews fall from the tree,
All the sighing on —and will not hush—
Some pleasant tales of thee.

JOHN CLARE

Maiden will you go with me,
Over land and over sea.

John Anderson

John Anderson my jo, John,
When we were first acquent,
Your locks were like the raven,
Your bonnie brow was brent;
But now your brow is beld, John,
Your locks are like the snow;
But blessings on your frosty pow,
John Anderson my jo.

John Anderson my jo, John,
We clamb the hill thegither,
And mony a canty day, John,
We've had wi' ane anither:
Now we maun totter down, John,
But hand in hand we'll go,
And sleep thegither at the foot,
John Anderson my jo.

ROBERT BURNS

Ne m'oubliez pas

REMEMBER ME

Remember me when I am gone away,
Gone far away into the silent land;
When you can no more hold me by the hand,
Nor I half turn to go, yet turning stay.
Remember me when no more day by day
You tell me of our future that you plann'd:
Only remember me; you understand
It will be late to counsel then or pray.
Yet if you should forget me for a while
And afterwards remember, do not grieve:
For if the darkness and corruption leave
A vestige of the thoughts that once I had,
Better by far you should forget and smile
Than that you should remember and be sad.

CHRISTINA GEORGINA ROSETTI

Red Red Rose

My love is like a red red rose
That's newly sprung in June:
My love is like the melody
That's sweetly play'd in tune.

As fair art thou, my bonnie lass,
So deep in love am I:
And I will love thee still, my dear,
Till a' the seas gang dry.

Till a' the seas gang dry, my dear,
And the rocks melt wi' the sun:
And I will love thee still, my dear,
While the sands o' life shall run.

And fare thee weel, my only love,
And fare thee weel a while!
And I will come again, my love,
Tho' it were ten thousand mile.

ROBERT BURNS

CHERRY

RIPE

There is a garden in her face
Where roses and white lilies blow;
A heavenly paradise is that place,
Wherein all pleasant fruits do flow:
There cherries grow which none may buy
Till 'Cherry-ripe' themselves do cry.

Those cherries fairly do enclose
Of orient pearls a double row,
Which when her lovely laughter shows,
They look like rose-buds filled with snow;
Yet them nor peer nor prince can buy
Till 'Cherry-ripe' themselves do cry.

Her eyes like angels watch them still;
Her brows like bended bows do stand,
Threat'ning with piercing frowns to kill
All that attempt with eye or hand
Those sacred cherries to come nigh,
Till 'Cherry-ripe' themselves do cry.

THOMAS CAMPION

[42]

Cherry
Hearts

Give
me,
love,
a word,
a sign

You
will be
my
Valen-
tine.

CUPID LOVES WINE.

The Vine

The wine of Love is music.
And the feast of Love is song:
And when Love sits down to the banquet,
Love sits long:

Sits long and arises drunken,
But not with the feast and the wine;
He reeleth with his own heart,
That great, rich Vine.

JAMES THOMSON

SONNET

Let me not to the marriage of true minds
Admit impediments. Love is not love
Which alters when it alteration finds,
Or bends with the remover to remove:
O, no! it is an ever-fixéd mark,
That looks on tempests and is never shaken;
It is the star to every wandering bark,
Whose worth's unknown, although his height be taken.
Love's not Time's fool, though rosy lips and cheeks
Within his bending sickle's compass come;
Love alters not with his brief hours and weeks,
But bears it out even to the edge of doom.
If this be error and upon me proved,
I never writ, nor no man ever loved.

WILLIAM SHAKESPEARE

With love and best wishes.

The editor wishes to express gratitude to The Mansell Collection and to the Mary Evans Picture Library for pictures reproduced in this book.